A Distinctive Approach

Modern Etiquette and Life Lessons for an Ever-Changing World

The Swann School of Protocol

WS Publishing

"A Distinctive Approach"

Published by WS Publishing, Carlsbad, California
www.ws-publishing.com

FIRST EDITION

Editor: Sopha Rosenzweig

Library of Congress Cataloging-in-Publication Data

The Swann School of Protocol

A Distinctive Approach: Modern Etiquette and Life Lessons for an Ever-Changing World/The Swann School of Protocol

p. cm.

ISBN-10: 0-9773520-8-0

ISBN-13: 978-0-9773520-8-1

Library of Congress Control Number: 2020924627

1.Self-Help 2. Business 3. Relationships

Scripture quotes taken from The Holy Bible: KING JAMES VERSION (KJV): KING JAMES VERSION, public domain

Printed in The United States of America

Be Well. Live Well.

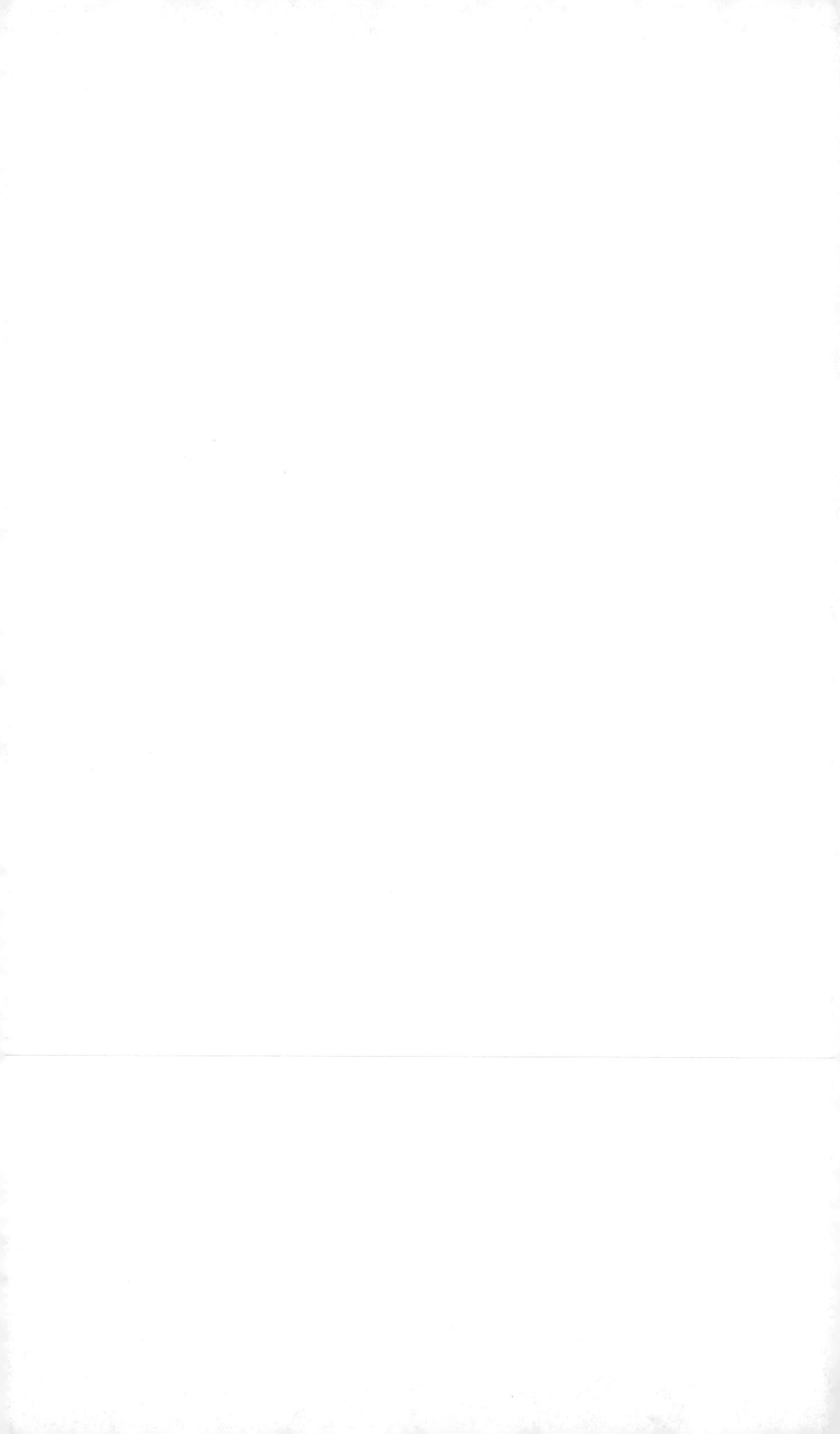

Table of Contents

Part One

A Distinctive Approach To

Self-Improvement

The Strength of a First Impression

Tisa Thompson

Making a good first impression is particularly important when it comes to meeting new people: like during an interview, meeting someone for the first time, or at a social gathering. These are the key points at which people will meet you and begin to form an impression of you. The quote "You make only one first impression" means that people decide what you're like before you say anything beyond your initial introduction. I've learned that first impressions are highly accurate in gauging a person's true personality and abilities. It turns out that you *can* judge a book by its cover after all.

Thus, mastering your first impression is not about hiding your true personality or trying to be someone you're not.

The goal of improving your conversational strategies and body language is simply to get these external behaviors to match and enhance, rather than contradict, your inner self. Even when you make a positive first impression, sometimes you're just not compatible with another person, and that is okay. You're not for everyone, and neither is anyone else.

When introducing yourself to someone: Stand, smile, and give a pleasant greeting and a firm handshake (web to web). Introduce yourself by name when you meet someone for the first time. If you're getting together with someone you haven't met before, introduce yourself by name and ask them what their name is. After they say their name, repeat it so you have a better chance of remembering it later. Offer your hand for a handshake (web to web) and use a firm hand grip, but not so firm that you hurt the person.

When introducing yourself:

a) State your first and last name.

b) Leave out your title, you don't want to appear pretentious. That information can be revealed at another time.

Concerning names:

a) Don't use first names until asked to do so or the other party immediately uses yours.

b) Forget a name? Just ask! You might even add, "In case you don't remember, my name is (<u>state your name</u>)." This will help take the edge off their possible embarrassment or disappointment in you not remembering their name.

c) If someone has a difficult name to pronounce, just ask them to repeat their name. If you expect to meet them again, you could ask for a business card.

Even when you make a positive
first impression,
sometimes you're just not
compatible with another person,
and that is okay.

The Power in a Voice

Dr. Tumona Austin

Find Your Voice

There will be times when you're misunderstood, misrepresented, unheard, and discounted. Take those challenges in stride and utilize them as a tool– an opportunity for learning and growth. Think of those situations as reminders for how much you have grown and how strong you are to have overcome such challenges and obstacles. When you have a clear understanding of who you are and what you represent, you can fully show up, exercise your voice, and stand in faith and confidence.

Everyone has a unique gift and special message. It's important that you're in touch with yourself and offer a consistent, authentic message. In order to effectively identify and exercise your voice, you must possess a level of self-awareness.

Get in touch with your mind, body, and soul through the practice of meditation. Spending time in silence, practicing mindfulness, and reflecting enables you to come into tune with your passions. Identify what it is that you do that you feel adds value. Become aware of what drives you to want to learn more and discover what gives you life. Self-discovery helps you find your inner voice, identify who you really are on the inside, and challenge the false beliefs that hold you back. You can also acquire a clear picture about what it is you desire in life to bring out the best in you.

Ask yourself this: *"If I don't know my voice (or platform), who is going to know it for me?"* Locate your voice and shift your focus from the past into the future. Be objective. Ask yourself pointed questions and be truthful. These questions should help you identify what you would do if you knew you could not fail, and what message you want to live on as your legacy.

Questions to consider:

1. How do you want the individuals you encounter to be different after you part ways?
2. What do you want to be associated with?
3. What is the one thing (hobby, cause, issue, etc.) that makes your heart beat?

It's important to dedicate time for self-reflection. Personal and professional growth are life-long journeys. You will learn many lessons across time. The one thing that will remain constant is that you're you, and no one can be a better you than yourself. Having said that, it's important to note that you will never be better at being anyone other than your true authentic self. You must believe that you have a seat at the table and that you're important, valued, and worthy. Affirm this belief to create the manifestation in your life.

Your voice is yours to own unapologetically and without fear!

- Lean into who you are.
- Embrace what you bring to the table.
- Walk in your brilliance.
- Share your blessings and valuable talents.

Know Your Audience

Now that you have discovered your voice, you're ready to be heard. In order to be heard, you must invest time and energy to identify your audience. Create a space and platform for your voice to be heard and received. The first step is getting to know your audience. Conduct research to become familiar with your audience. This enables you to connect with them on a deeper level and create a safe space to be open and transparent. Share some of yourself. While researching your audience, some things to consider are:

1. What are their values, ideals, goals, aspirations, and dreams?
2. What makes them unique?
3. What circumstances or challenges are they looking to overcome (or have already overcome)?

Icebreakers are a useful tool to quickly and effectively learn about others. FORM is an acronym commonly utilized in the military that stands for: Family/Friends, Occupation, Recreation and Motivation. FORD is a variation of FORM and stands for: Family/Friends, Occupation, Recreation, Dreams. FORM is a methodological series of specific prompts to open up lines of conversation while avoiding awkward moments of silence. FORM enables you to get to know people better and keep the conversation alive without being intrusive. It also helps you avoid hot topics (i.e. politics and religion).

It's essential to establish your voice, as you don't want to unintentionally take on somebody else's voice. Taking on someone else's voice can damage your brand, call your integrity into question, and temporarily derail you from your goals and aspirations. You worked hard to be viewed as credible, knowledgeable, and trustworthy. Your voice, your message, your story, and your inner light can help others discover and embrace their own voice.

Self-discovery helps you find
your inner voice,
identify who you really are on
the inside, and challenge the
false beliefs that hold you back.

The Grace in a Tone

Nikesha Tannehill Tyson

Set yourself apart with Grace and Kindness

Be brutally honest without being brutal – Honesty is one of the three core values of etiquette.

"It's not what you say, it's how you say it." This is a statement that we've heard so many times, and it still rings true today. Getting your point across is easy when using kind words and phrases. Words have so much power. They can put a smile on someone's face, bring tears, or cause an old wound to resurface.

Recognizing your tone while speaking can be a challenge to process. Have someone whom you trust to randomly record some of your encounters and review it with you. Think of it this way, if the words you speak were the last words someone heard, would you be pleased?

A young lady helped me realize how powerful kind words and phrases can be. Someone is always watching or listening, even when you don't realize it. A past incident brought this full circle for me, and here's what happened:

An employee came in, I noticed that he was a few minutes late. Instead of reporting to his assigned location for duty, he decided to review schedules to determine breaks and lunches for himself as well as other employees. I said, "Hello, how are you today?" I waited for a reply. Then, I added, "You're a bit behind today, and someone is waiting for you to relieve them. Please take care of the person that should be relieved from their duties, and you're welcome to review the schedule during your scheduled breaks or lunch." I also thanked him. He replied, "Yes, ma'am." Another employee noticed the exchange and replied, "You just checked him, and he will never know it. Now, allow that to sink in."

I must say, her response taught me the value of consideration and respect while being polite in conversation.

So, it worked! There is power in being polite. That power can yield the desired outcome in any situation.

Words have so much power.
They can put a smile
on someone's face, bring tears,
or cause an old wound to
resurface.

The Humility in an Online Presence

Elaine Swann

We've all seen it; you log onto Facebook or Instagram and see a post of a friend posing next to his BMW. He says the picture is about the beach, but we all know that the waves only serve as the backdrop for the beaming beamer that is front and center in the post. The act is called humblebragging, and practically all of us have been guilty of it at some point.

What is Humblebragging?

Humblebragging is a sly way of talking about your life, in all its greatness, online. You're sharing bits and pieces of your life, but at the same time, you're bragging. Now, don't misconstrue the idea, because social media is meant for sharing milestones. Humblebragging, however, are those posts on Facebook or Twitter that tells the world how great your life is in a downplayed sort of way.

For Example...

A person will post, "Oh gosh, just got sand all over the carpet of my brand-new BMW." The purpose here is to draw attention to the BMW, not the sand. Such bragging also takes place when someone takes a photo of their nails resting on or near the Mercedes-Benz emblem on their car's steering wheel.

What's So Wrong with Humblebragging?

It's not horrible to share accomplishments online. You just have to be realistic. Ask yourself: *"What's my key point here? Do I want to complain about the sand? Or do I want people to know about my BMW?"* If you want people to know about your car, then just be forward with it and say, "I'm so thankful that I've a BMW. I always dreamed of having this kind of car." Humblebragging gets annoying when a person does it often, so it's best to be honest and upfront.

Also, bragging should not be done often. Your accomplishments should not be something that you're always discussing online. You want to think about your audience and who's reading the posts. If you just got a brand-new BMW and most of the people you associate with are not necessarily in that space, then you probably want to hold back a little bit and not talk about it all the time.

Questions to Consider Before Posting

1. What is this post all about? Is the post really about the sand or is it about the BMW?
2. Is this something I've mentioned before?
3. How would my community feel about what I'm sharing? Would it make them feel good about their personal situation or bad?
4. Is there a way that I can share this differently by being more upfront?

You can spot humblebragging when a person is making one minuscule thing, but they really want to shed light on it. If you do catch someone engaging in humblebragging red-handed—just ignore it. Don't try to correct them. Just Let Crazy Be Crazy and leave them alone!

Just Let Crazy Be Crazy

and leave them alone!

Part Two

A Distinctive Approach To

Family

The Effects of a Dream

Britney Lowery

People that have left a footprint that has surpassed their time on Earth, did not do so by mistake. They were clear on setting their goal, committing to the work, and raising the standard for those that were set to follow behind them. Etiquette offers a framework, to build on on any economic, family, or societal history tree. If used properly, knowing the language of etiquette can strategically align your core values around

Consideration, Honesty, and Respect while effortlessly purifying your pursuits in your business, community, and personal efforts.

One of the primary directives of etiquette and protocol is for you to look past yourself. The idea of manners is not to maintain your own comfort but instead to consider the ease of those around you. When building a dream and exploring your imagination, use this same instruction to navigate to get the most out of any opportunity. What good is a dream that is only sufficient to propel you? What purpose does imagination have if it doesn't push you to stretch your starting limits? If your ideas don't scare you, then you're not thinking big enough.

Consider the first organization ever built: Family. Varying from the traditional father, mother, and child(ren) to career-focused couples, tight-knit siblings, single parents, and multi-generational households, everyone in that unit plays a vital role. Just as important as their role is, so are their actions—everything that each individual does will affect the others. Whether they are aware of it or not, they each pave a legacy of character, wisdom, or even love.

Etiquette offers a framework of this simple law of nature—everything that you do causes a ripple, directly or indirectly affecting those around you. You will realize that you must decide what it is that you're going to leave behind after you're no longer here.

Having been raised by creative parents—my father was a brick mason and architect while my mother was a graphic designer and drawing artist—I knew early on that I had the right to create whatever I wanted, including my future.

Things did not just happen to me, instead, life responded to my design. Whether it was the atmosphere of a room or the outcome of a job interview, I understood that every action I took acted as a seed ensuring that I had a say-so in what the future held. As a descendant of the Creator, according to Genesis 1:27, (So God created man in his own image, in the image of God created he him; male and female created he them), you have the right to ignite your surroundings to work in your favor and set a better foundation for those who are to come after you.

This is no campaign to instruct anyone to be completely selfless. However, the things in the realm of your dreams, goals, and imagination should act as a fertilizer for your future self, those around you, and even for those you're not aware of.

As a mother, I've learned a sure thing about children: they are completely fearless. They jump off things not knowing how they will land, they sing loudly without any notice of who will hear them or what they will disrupt, and they want to eat whatever they crave without any calorie-count.

The most fascinating thing for me was to see my daughter learn to walk. She simply got up and gave it a try. Time after time, she kept trying without any Life Coach appointments, Motivational Monday hashtags, or self-help books. She watched those around her use their legs to get them anywhere from the kitchen to the car to the mailbox. She made up in her mind that she had the untapped potential of walking. As she got to the point of walking more than just a few steps, the joy in her face could light up a room.

She did not care about my laughing tears or the iPhone recording I was taking of her; she was filled with her own success of walking. But not long after, while I was still telling the world of this grand benchmark, she refreshed her pursuits to running. While it's good to celebrate, it's easy to soak too long in the champagne and glitter of a met goal. Do a victory dance and use the momentum to offset your next goal.

Language is not just the dialect of the words you utter, it's a lifestyle of Consideration, Honor, and Respect. Long before you enter a room or begin the introductory part of an interview, your mindset and heart posture has already gone before you to introduce you. I invite you to take on the most valuable principle of etiquette: always consider that everything you do affects everything and everyone around you.

The Foundation of Parenting

Tisa Thompson

As parents, we never know what road our child will take. But we must always communicate effectively with our children. The way we speak to our children has a significant impact on their learning and ability to listen to us. At all times, we must be the model to our children on how to act and behave. When speaking to your child use: your child's name, positive language, appropriate volume, model and expect good manners, be considerate (don't interrupt), show acceptance, and make conversation a priority with your child.

Helping young children learn appropriate, polite, and considerate behaviors enables them to form good manners and become more socially attentive as they get older. It's easier to nurture superb child behavior if you work as a family to set the rules/guidelines for good manners in many different situations. You never know who you're raising. You could be raising the future president of the United States.

As parents, we must "speak life into our children." Speak words of praise, gratitude, validation, honor, and encouragement. Some of the values you may teach your children include kindness, manners, and consideration of other people. For example, the three core values of kindness and good manners are: respect, honesty, and consideration.

1. You should respect others even if you don't get along.
2. It's important to understand that not everyone will be your best friend, but you must always be kind to those around you.
3. Be brave and stand up for yourself and others when they are being treated badly.
4. Before you make a choice to act or speak, always consider how the other person might feel.

Consideration Towards Others

1. Always use kind words such as "Please" and "Thank you," and use them every day.
2. Be polite to people who have jobs that help you such as the grocery clerk, the lunch lady, the bus driver, and more.
3. If you see someone in need of help, step in and help!
4. It's nice to be polite to people you don't know.
5. Be careful in what you say to and about people who look different than you.
6. Try not to stare at people who are overweight or disabled.
7. If you want to ask your parent a question about the way someone acts or looks, wait until you're alone.
8. Always practice patience. Wait your turn at school, at home, and when out and about.
9. When you're waiting in a line, sometimes it's nice to let people go ahead of you.

Good manners are important to have since they show that you're courteous to other people. Having good social etiquette can help you develop better relationships and make you more enjoyable to be around. If you're having a meal with others, make sure you use good manners while you're eating to show that you're respectful. You also should maintain etiquette, so you don't offend or overshare with others. Use "please" and "thank you" when you're asking for something. These two words will take your child the farthest in life.

For example, you may say, "Can you please point me in the direction of the bread?" Once you're given direction, say, "Thank you."

When addressing elders, persons of authority, mentors, parents, etc., address them as "Ma'am" or "Sir." As simple as it may sound, no matter the situation, kindness is always appropriate.

Children can be opinionated. They are learning about the world and forming independent thoughts and ideas, so there may be times that they express their opinions, and it comes across in a rude way. Everyone is entitled to an opinion, but that doesn't mean a teen should be rude. We must teach our teenagers to share their opinions in a respectful manner to avoid coming across as overbearing, pushy, or just rude in general.

Good manners are used EVERYWHERE, not just at home or on special occasions. Make good manners a habit at home so that you can use them everywhere.

At the movie theater:

1. Don't put your feet on the seat, kick the seat in front of you, or keep getting up and out of your seat.

2. If you do get up, be polite and say, "Excuse me."
3. Be mindful of any bags or backpacks. Make sure your items don't hit other people as you pass by.
4. If someone else is trying to pass by, stand and push up your seat back. Don't just move your legs.

In Waiting Rooms (doctor's office, dentist, hospitals, airports and more):

1. Bring something to read or a quiet game.
2. Don't disturb other people by talking and asking too many questions.
3. Always speak quietly or in a normal tone of voice.

Traveling:

Cars

1. Sit forward in the seat.
2. Fasten your seatbelt.
3. Keep your feet and hands inside the car.
4. Ask if it's okay to open the window.

Airplanes

1. Don't talk too loudly.

2. Don't kick the seat in front of you.
3. Don't play your music too loud.
4. Don't turn your light off and on too often.
5. Don't keep adjusting your seat back and forth.

The fantastic thing is, if you give your child these simple tools, you will be amazed at the positive difference it makes in their ease of navigating the world around them.

The Gratitude from Mindfulness

Tisa Thompson

The first thing to remember is that teenagers' unique developmental task is to individuate—to break away from you, the parent, who is looking for a little appreciation. We want to feel more gratitude, and we want our kids to do the same, because gratitude is so closely associated with happiness that the two are practically indistinguishable from one another.

The opposite of gratitude is entitlement, which brings negative feelings like disappointment and frustration. When we feel grateful, our world fills with positive emotions like love, compassion, enthusiasm, and confidence—and our satisfaction with life soars.

It's not until later in life that most people discover that gratitude is one of the keys to happiness. The concept of thankfulness can be difficult for adults to embrace and even harder for children and teens who believe the world revolves around them. When gratitude is modeled, it's not just a lesson to be taught to the child, but an ongoing exercise in learning for the parent.

Instead of idolizing the newest gadget, work on being grateful for what you have right now. When interacting with your children, share frequently and generously, and say "please" and "thank you" so that good manners are *what we do* and not just what we say. Be mindful of your time spent. Take time to appreciate the sights, smells and sounds around you, and you'll model mindfulness for your kids.

Research suggests that happiness is, in fact, less the result of circumstance and more the product of our own thinking and habits. In other words, you don't have to wait until you have the perfect life to be happy. While it can be difficult to choose happiness in tough times such as, during the COVID-19 pandemic. You can choose it right now by focusing on what you're grateful for and encouraging your children to do the same.

When gratitude is modeled, it's not just a lesson to be taught to the child, but an ongoing exercise in learning for the parent.

Part Three

A Distinctive Approach To

Healthy Relationships

The Investment in Interpersonal Relationships

Lynette Lealwalcott

Relationship Etiquette for Your Daily Interactions

As you can see as it relates to the topic of etiquette there are a plethora of areas in which we could investigate that would help us to become a better version of ourselves. Let me now walk you through some areas as it relates to relationship etiquette. No, not the mushy, touchy boyfriend/girlfriend type, but your day-to-day relationships. Relationships are the foundation of everything we involve ourselves in. How we cultivate or handle our relationships will have a great impact on the course of our life being positive or negative.

How many times have you encountered someone and sometime throughout the course of the relationship, however long or short it may be, things began to feel a bit awkward? Are you friends, acquaintances, strangers passing through the course of life, or is this a simple exchange fulfilling a specific need at this point in life? Regardless of the nature of the relationship, there is always a way to interact with other people that will show an authentic kindness and thoughtfulness towards them. It should always be your goal that when someone leaves your presence, they generally felt that they mattered. This should be the case during cordial moments and times of conflict.

1. Be honest about the relationship

I'm sure that many of you have heard the quote, “People come into your life for a reason, a season, or a lifetime. When you figure out which one it is, you will know what to do for each person.” I would propose to you that you be upfront about your intentions.

Say your son went to a birthday party and his friend's mom made an amazing birthday cake. Your son's birthday is in a few months, and you just have to have her make a cake. Why go through all the hassle of arranging playdates just to get in with her to make a cake when you have no intention of befriending her as an individual? The polite and mature thing to do would be to be up front. You should compliment her on the amazing job she did on the cake and express your interest in having her make a cake for your son's upcoming party. Should friendship develop from there, you have indeed gained a true friendship. You should never use relationships as manipulation to simply get what you want. This goes against etiquette core values and putting others at ease.

2. It's all about delivery

Now, you may ask, what about the times where there was an established relationship foundation, and the expectation is greater? It can be difficult when working on a simple project together turns into coffee dates, or afternoon lunch invites. I mean the project is long over, or so you thought it was. Be mindful to not allow yourself to go with the flow out of obligation. Always remain present with your goals and ambitions, or you can easily find yourself losing time, and become way off track. You must learn the power of NO and be able to deliver your position in a polite, yet firm way.

Always lead with a positive.

For example, "I've thoroughly enjoyed the time we've spent together, and the project was a huge success." Then, follow with a moving challenge and encouragement for the both of you. Example, "I'm sure we could go on and on, however, I know we both have some other things we need to focus on to reach our next level of success and happiness." Finally, you must close to put the unspoken expectation in its place. Example, "It's been great, however, now it's time for me to buckle down on some other things. Should our paths cross in the future I'm sure it will be great. I wish you the best."

In this delivery you're expressing appreciation and gratitude. This will get your point across in a way of understanding. It's not too harsh nor are you just avoiding an individual. It's important that you take the time and keep everything in its place.

3. Remember ownership on both sides of the relationship

This leads into our last point that responsibility lies on both individuals involved. It's damaging to go into a relationship with assumptions or to be hoping and wishing. Living a life of purpose means to be intentional in all areas of life, including relationship.

Understanding that it can be risky to take on the responsibility and ownership of navigating a relationship can make one feel vulnerable. This vulnerability is the foundation of what the relationship is being built upon, therefore, it's worth the risk. We're the navigators of our lives and with that, we do owe it to others that we make connections with, that we don't stir them wrong. Imagine you have a boat and invited some friends for a nice afternoon on the lake. Friends arrive and you charge one of them to be captain with no direction or expectation. If the afternoon turns into a complete disaster, this disaster would fall on you, because you failed to take ownership and be responsible. The same would go for relationships. The expectation of a relationship is the responsibility of each individual. The biblical Proverbs says, "if the blind lead the blind, both shall fall into a ditch," Matthew 15:14.

Don't find yourself trying to climb out of the bad situation by trying to be too nice in relationships. Etiquette doesn't mean yielding your right to speak up. In fact, it means to absolutely speak up with grace and kindness.

Develop Your Communication

1. Talk vs texting

With most of the world having cell phones and other technology, we've somewhat lost the art of talking to each other. I mean, we could just as easily shoot a quick text and be about our merry way. As stated before, etiquette is about making the other person feel comfortable and being clear in our intentions. With The Swann School of Protocol's three core values being respect, honesty and consideration; we can't always get these across through a simple text message. It's important to know when to pick up the phone or have a face-to-face conversation.

A text message can be void of feeling, leaving the receiver to interpret its meaning through their own filters. It can also be viewed as avoidance depending on the nature of conversation. This is not a good foundation for a relationship because it leaves too much unsaid while you're really wanting to build a relationship on honesty and intimacy.

There is much to gain through personal interaction with another person that can't be achieved through text. We communicate through our body language, the tone of our voice, and so much more, that make up our individual persons. These things are what gives our words feeling and life and produce a direction and a hope. There is a time for text messaging, and it just shouldn't be replaced for a conversation of meaning.

2. Don't move so fast, take your time

Along with living in a society that will send a text before talking face-to-face, we're met with living in a microwave society. This has really impacted the way we interact and deal with each other as individuals. This is probably why it's so hard to make that phone call or schedule that face to face because it may take more time than we're willing to set aside. I implore you to consider slowing down in your day to day and especially when dealing with people. We miss so much when we can't stop for a minute.

Have you ever experienced having a conversation with someone and feeling like it's going into one ear and out the other? You question if they're even hearing a word you're saying, period. I mean to the point that you want to ask them to repeat the conversation back to you. Well, this is our day-to-day when we move so fast. We end the day with the question, what did I even do today?

To really develop proper relationships, we have to take our time. It means a great deal to give another person your undivided attention, look them in the eyes while communicating, or actually turn your phone off. This is giving great consideration. This is letting another person know that they matter and whatever your involvement is with them, it takes precedence in that time.

When we take our time, we're acknowledging the present. Acknowledging the present gives us time to evaluate what we really want or what we can really do. Finally, knowing those things yield purposeful relationships and destiny. It's okay to be the tortoise, I'm sure he took in a lot more of the journey than the hair did.

3. How to break the ice

Now that you've slowed down, you run into a stranger, or assigned a new doctor, or interviewing a new company to partner with. How are you going to break the ice to even begin building a relationship?

The first thing in breaking the ice is to make yourself friendly. You must be relatable, vulnerable, and authentic. Start your conversation with something you feel comfortable opening up about that they may relate to or know something about them that you can relate to so that you can have a general conversation. If you're wanting to build a lasting relationship, it's important to allow people to see the genuine you outside of the business briefcase. It's important to make the individual feel at ease. You can do this by asking open ended questions, and this will give them the opportunity to speak.

As you listen intently, you're listening for something in which you can connect with that will result in a sincere conversation. This will bring walls and guards down. Be considerate, respectful, and honest. In a few minutes time, this individual that was a complete stranger has now become someone that you're having a substantive conversation with, and it feels as if you've known each other for years.

How to Interact with People in Your Everyday Life

1. Strangers

Learning how to break the ice should not be mistaken for interacting and dealing with all people in the same way. We should interact with others according to their place in our life. Let's look at a few different situations.

A complete stranger should always be dealt with in a kind manner. We meet strangers unaware, not knowing if they are brought into our lives for a specific reason or if the simple smile on our face was what they needed to see the beauty in the day.

Oftentimes people will not interact with strangers and opt to keep to themselves. This leaves us lacking a great gratitude because it's natural in our human nature to be social. Rejection and society have caused us to force a blind eye to the stranger doing ourselves and them an injustice. Shirley MacLaine states that, "fear make strangers of friends." Push the fear aside and start with a smile and hello. Give others and yourself the opportunity to deposit a pleasant gratitude in each other's course of the day.

2. Friends

When we're dealing with friends, a quote from my brother, Samuel Giles, comes to mind, "Give space for grace in every case." We must be mindful to not become too comfortable or familiar in our friendships that we're no longer a true friend. In friendship, we must take time to make the relationship priority without causing or responding to unrealistic expectations. There is a wealth in friendship that is unmatched if we nurture and respect the relationship as we do ourselves. Many things will fade and change over the course of our lives; however, a true friendship will last the course of a lifetime.

The Swann School of Protocol's three core values really are the foundation of friendship.

Respect: while interacting with a friend, it's important to respect their stage within their life. You should respect their space and be secure enough in your friendship that you might not talk every day and that's okay.

Honesty: we should always be honest with a friend. It can be good, bad, or indifferent, however, we should not fear being honest. Honesty is what bonds the relationship.

Consideration: yes, there are many times in a friendship where you will need to consider them over yourself. The intimacy of friendship will allow you to see into them and what they need at a certain point in life and the depth of that relationship will cause you to yield to that need.

Friendships are key. We may be on a quest to acquire many things, but the real beauty in this life is our individual character and the memory of relationships that we leave with others.

3. Essential service workers

Finally, I would like to touch on how we should interact with people that are in essential service to others. We can often overlook or pass them by, however, they are deserving of that "slow down" we talked about earlier. This is an area where the "please" and "thank you" of etiquette can go a long way.

The question, "How may I be of service to you?" is a good approach in dealing with this group of individuals. Your service may simply be by asking how their day is going. By simply acknowledging them as individuals in one form or manner you can take their mind off the continual service and elevate them back to their why (meaning, why they chose to do what they do). We should never take their service for granted and from time to time find a random act of kindness to make them smile.

Find a way to express gratitude from a genuine place of love and appreciation. Gratitude improves the relationship for them as well as for yourself.

It can be easy to feel like others know that we're grateful for what they do, however, going the extra step and letting others know that you value their efforts will actually deepen their commitment and build a stronger community.

Let's not overlook the essential workers that serve as we're learning about relationship etiquette. We should invest in these relationships in word and in deed. Purposeful, intentional, and healthy relationships make for a healthier overall life.

Be honest, considerate, and respectful in all relationships.

Acknowledging the present
gives us time to
evaluate what we really want or
what we can really do.

The Clarity for the Entanglements of Dating Life

Desiree Hunter

Online Dating

Ahhh, the wonders of online dating.

That beautiful, exciting dance between two strangers who go from matching to meeting to matrimony.

That is how it always goes, right? *Sigh*. Sadly, not so much.

But online dating doesn't have to be a drag. In fact, it can be downright delightful.

Not only are the number of marriages resulting from relationships that started online increasing every year, but studies have also found these matches have a higher success rate!

We've come a long way from when the online dating universe was looked upon as a wasteland for lonely singles. These days you can match, swipe, and click your way to love from literally anywhere.

In this chapter, we'll be going over dating etiquette and discussing do's, don'ts, and some common dilemmas that can pop up in the romance realm.

Over the past few years, I've had the pleasure of interviewing dozens of people on their dating journeys and will be sharing some of their experiences and insights with you in this chapter, which is taken from my book, "Legs Closed, Heart Open."

It's important to note that for these purposes, I'll be defaulting to heterosexual relationships/couples where the man is most comfortable in the masculine energy role and the woman's dominant energy is feminine. However, this dating etiquette applies to couples where one partner relates most to traditional ideas of masculine energy and the other partner relates most to traditional ideas of feminine energy.

We can look at these energies from the biological standpoint as well by observing the egg, which is stationary and in receiving mode; and the sperm, which is active and in the pursuer mode.

Feminine = Calm, Restful, Slow, Receiving (Egg)

Masculine = Busy, Action, Doing, Giving (Sperm)

Here is a fun fact! Lest we write off the egg or feminine energy as being passive and helpless, researchers have found that the egg emits chemical signals that attract and guide certain sperm over to them.

Talk about powerful feminine energy!

There is a little something I would like to get off my chest regarding feminism, femininity, and modern vs. traditional relationships. I'm not sure why, but there is a tendency to think feminism and being feminine are two different things and that they are at odds with each other. I think we should all be feminists in that feminism is simply the belief that women are no less valuable than men. So, women should be afforded the same rights, we should be paid equally (which, we're still not), and we should not be discriminated against or viewed as less than men.

However, it's important to acknowledge that while We're indeed equal, men and women are NOT the same. Those contrasts should be celebrated and not downplayed, denied, or ignored. Men and women *are* DIFFERENT and that is a great thing! Our pie charts both add up to 100%, yet the way the pie is distributed is unique and distinct. Side note: Both pies are still incredibly delicious.

Women: we're magic. Don't forget that. Know your worth and conduct yourself as such.

Men: Women are magic. Don't forget that. Know our worth and conduct yourself as such.

I know a lot of the traditional way of approaching dating and relationships has fallen by the wayside, but I don't think We've to leave things that way. In fact, I'm convinced that our overall satisfaction in our romantic relationships will increase with a return to some of the "ways of old."

Chivalry goes a very, very long way. I can't stress this enough. So, men, if you're ever in doubt, just think of what the gentlemanly thing to do would be and do that.

On the flip side ladies, when in doubt, go the feminine route and think of these quotes from Coco Chanel: "A woman can be overdressed but never over elegant," and "A girl should be two things: classy and fabulous."

Lean towards the side of elegance and class.

Overall Etiquette: A Quick Note

I would be remiss to just jump into dating etiquette without first talking about overall etiquette. The truth is overall etiquette IS dating etiquette! We'll get into this more in the next sections, of course, but manners that you would use on a day-to-day basis should most definitely be transferred to dating.

The Golden Rule is golden *everywhere* and even more so in the minefield that can be dating. Your actions have an effect (in some cases long-term) on those you date and interact with, so take extra care to avoid doing harm whenever possible. Remember, the actions of those who are going out dating today play a role in the experiences of someone's future husband or wife, including your own.

With that said, let's get into it!

Getting to Know You: Matching & Messaging

Love at First Swipe

Most dating apps these days have a "swiping" feature including, the juggernaut Tinder, which introduced the now ubiquitous "swipe."

How it works is users swipe Left for No and Right for Yes when reviewing profiles of prospective dates. Tinder developers say they came up with the concept because they wanted to add a "game-like" element to the app, which does two things: it makes swiping on a match feel like you have won something; and it also keeps you on the app for longer periods of time, which the developers (and their advertisers, no doubt) appreciate.

The swiping concept does indeed feel like a game. Once you swipe right on someone who also swiped Yes for you, a big green "You Matched!" pops up on the screen and you get a twinge of satisfaction. With most sites, it's only when you have matched with someone that you can send them a message.

So, you've matched! Congratulations. Now comes the hard part—What to say.

Mister & Miss-Represented, A Picture is Worth a Thousand Words

This next segment has got to be one of the most common pet peeves or complaints that I hear from folks. Women seem to be the bigger offenders in this area, but there are most certainly men who are guilty of this too—misrepresenting yourself in pictures. This could mean photos that are 30 pounds and ten years away from what you currently look like.

This is flabbergasting to me because you're planning to meet people in person at some point, right? Unless you're planning to grow another three inches or drop a good 20 pounds in the week or two that it takes to meet up, why in the world would you put up misleading pictures? Out of all the men I've interviewed, not one of them has said they continued to date a woman who had effectively lied by putting up pictures that were different than what she actually looked like. In a nutshell, doing so makes men feel duped, lied to, bamboozled, and hoodwinked and they are right to feel that way.

"She was actually cool and was still very pretty even though she was much heavier than in her pictures," one guy said. "Even though I liked her, and we had a good time, things just couldn't move on from there because I felt like she lied to me from the beginning. And if she's lying about how she looks, what else is she lying about?"

I asked one guy what his number one tip would be for women and here's what he said:

"I wish women would realize that they're beautiful. That whatever it is they think they need to change about themselves, there is a man who loves whatever it's they're wanting to change. They should embrace themselves and just be themselves, so that way, they will find a man who is looking for them instead of who they're pretending to be."

Bottom line is this: you're doing way more harm than good with "catfish-lite" pictures. Always put up accurate shots that showcase your beautiful self! Men, the issue with your pictures tend to be group shots, baseball caps and sunglasses. You want to have the majority of your pictures without these items and without other people. Have at least one close-up, one head and shoulders, and one full-body picture. Lose the angles (everyone has caught on to that little trick anyways), duck lips, and shirtless bathroom selfies. Also, be mindful of what is in the background of your pictures, whether it be a messy room or risqué painting or a pet that is in the process of making a pit stop. You want the attention to be on you, not what is in the background.

Say cheese and have fun!

Messaging

For women or those who are primarily in their feminine energy, I recommend not messaging first. By matching, you have already shown that you're interested. So, it's okay to lean back and wait for the masculine person to do their thing, which is to act. I like to think of it this way: The Masculine acts and The Feminine reacts.

Some apps have features like "winks," "pokes," or "likes," which are little things that you can do to show interest. Ladies, these are okay to do once, maybe twice at the very most, but the first message should be left up to the man.

Men, I know it's a bummer and the vast majority of your messages will likely not get a response (more on how to increase your chances of getting a reply to come). However, messaging a woman first shows that you can take initiative and go after what (or in this case who) you want. I can tell you as a woman who is more on the traditional side of things, this is very much noticed and appreciated. Being able to send an intelligent message is one of the very first signs for a woman to see you're a man of value who knows and embraces his masculine role as a "doer."

With the Bumble app, one of the key features is that women are the ones who must send the first message after matching. Even with this, ladies, you can keep that initial message to a short, "Hi James, I'm glad we matched!" and let the guy take it from there.

You will soon find with online dating that you will be inundated with potential suitors. After a while, you're almost looking for reasons to strike folks from the running and thin the herd. Men, that means while you don't want to obsess over that first missive, it's important, and if you're shooting your shot, you want to have your best chance of getting a response back.

Right off the bat, clearly copied and pasted messages are a "no-no" and, for me, are the easiest ones to dismiss along with time wasters like: "Hi," "How are you," "My name is -------," "Happy -insert day of the week here-," "How's your -insert day of the week here- going?" "Do you like -insert ethnic group- guys?" etc.

When it comes to messaging, try not to do too much too soon or get too familiar with a person. Think of it as how you would do introductions if you met someone in real life (IRL). Chances are, you would not just walk up to someone and say, "Hi, beautiful," or "Hi, sexy," or "Hi, handsome." So, approach your online openings and early conversations the same way.

In general, pet names like sweetheart, babe, etc. should be avoided until much later in the relationship when both parties are comfortable. Remember, these are terms of endearment so don't use them until there is some endearing going on!

So, what should men say in a first message?

After consulting with several women, the consensus seems to fall around three keys:

Keep it short and sweet (KISS)

1. Mention something specific to them and their profile to show you actually read what they wrote.
2. Ask a question to keep the conversation going.

Studies show that women get more messages than men, by far. Ladies, I know it can be daunting to respond to everyone. And, in some cases, it's simply not possible. Even though you're only getting messages from those you have matched with, it's inevitable that sometimes you will match only to go back and really read their profiles and discover there is some reason why you're not well suited after all. When the man sends a "throw-away" message like those outlined above, it's easy to do just that–throw them away. If he could not take the time and energy to invest in a legit message, then you don't need to worry or feel guilty about not sending a response.

But what about those cases when he does take the time? It's a witty, well thought-out message that is short, sweet and does all the right things. Is it rude to leave those messages unanswered and ignored? Well, men seem to be torn on the issue, but here's my take:

In those cases, I still respond and thank them for their message, noting how good it made me feel to get it. "Hi Guy, thanks for your note, it always feels good to get a thoughtful message on here! After taking a closer look at your profile, it looks like we wouldn't be a good romantic match after all. But thanks again, and all the best!"

Men, try not to take it personally and just simply chalk it up to one of those unfair things in life. Your messages many times go unanswered in online dating and women still only make 80 cents or less to every dollar a man makes. See? Life is not always fair. ;)

Let's Make a Date

After exchanging a few messages back and forth, it's time to remove the "online" from dating and just meet up! Set up a coffee meeting. If you do want to have a quick phone chat beforehand, that works too. Just by all means, avoid a prolonged chat and text fest with someone you've never actually met in person. That's a recipe for catfish for sure.

I like to say meet online then immediately get offline! Nothing matters until you meet in person anyway, so why put that off?

Guys, it's still okay to ask for a woman's number. In fact, it's preferred.

One of my pet peeves is when a man just sends his number with the instructions to call him. If...no, let's make that a strong ***IF*** We've had a good exchange and I'm genuinely intrigued by him, then I'll respond with, "Great! I'm at 111-222-3345 and am generally available from 6-8 pm on weekdays, hope you have a great day!" and return the ball squarely back to his court.

If I was already just "meh" about him, well, there is a good chance his number would just sit there.

There used to be a "three-day" rule when the parties involved were instructed to wait three days before calling, lest they look thirsty. Well, with the way our shortened attention spans are set up now, those days are gone! I would not say to call or text immediately after getting someone's number, but don't feel like you have to wait three whole days! My advice for men is to call or text within a day or so after getting a woman's number, at least just to touch base.

Once a date has been arranged, try your very best not to cancel or reschedule. If doing so is absolutely unavoidable, give them as much notice as possible and be proactive in figuring out alternate days/times.

I generally advise people to keep first meetings to 30 minutes or so to just grab a cup of coffee and basically confirm your and your date's identity. If that one goes well, THEN you can make plans for a proper date. Here is a tip for that first coffee meeting: Order a medium size cold drink. This way, you can nurse it if things are going well and you want to prolong the meeting, or you can chug it down and politely excuse yourself when the meeting (and your drink) comes to an end.

Getting to know you DO's:

- Men, do send a KISS message (as explained a couple pages back) to a woman first and when it comes to that time in the conversation, do ask for her phone number.
- Do keep your first meeting to something small—think 30 minutes and a $5 cup of coffee.
- Do be honest with your pictures and only post those that truly represent your current appearance.

Getting to know you DON'Ts:

- Men, after getting the number of the person you're interested in, don't feel like you have to wait three days to call them.
- Don't get too familiar and reveal too many personal details too soon–leave the pet names for much later in the relationship.
- Don't misrepresent yourself. (Yes, this is worth repeating!) I know there is pressure to be something you think someone will like, but it's better to be yourself from the start so you will attract a partner who is looking for someone exactly like you.

During the Date: Dress, Dine & Discuss

Dress

This is really going to depend on what your first date activity will be, but no matter what you're doing, wear something that makes you feel good, comfortable, and confident. Dress in what is appropriate for the activity. For example, don't wear sneakers on an outing to a nice restaurant or heels for a hike. If you're not sure about what to wear: ladies, you can never go wrong with a nice dress that you can style up or down; and men, a dress shirt and nice pair of jeans are a safe go-to.

For a first date, it's recommended you meet at a public place and arrive there separately. It doesn't matter how long you have spent chatting online, on the phone, or on FaceTime, etc. YOU STILL DON'T KNOW THIS PERSON. It's easy to get carried away and too comfortable too soon (which is why I don't recommend spending too much time chatting before meeting). For the safety of everyone involved, never forget that this person is still a stranger who you're getting to know. That means meeting in well-populated public places, not going in their cars with them, and definitely not going to each other's homes prematurely. If it helps you, watch a few episodes of "Law & Order: SVU" to bring home the reminder that there are bad people out there, then do so. I would suggest watching "Dateline" or "First 48" too, but then you might just give up dating entirely!

For the sake of our purposes, let us say the first date location is a restaurant. Keep in mind that in my approach you would have already met for coffee, and this would be your first "real" date. Gentlemen, find out what type of food your date is partial to and suggest 2-3 options that are in her area since you're going to want to drive to her part of town. Ladies, if the man asks you to drive to him or asks you to choose someplace, then let him know you would prefer for the gentleman to plan the date. You can say something like, "I'm excited to meet up with you and it makes me feel good when a gentleman plans the date. Some of what I enjoy is Italian food and seafood and I live in (city) so any place within that general vicinity works for me. I'm sure whatever you decide will be great!"

Men, since you will be paying for this outing, (I hope that doesn't come as a shocker) be sure to check the menus and price points ahead of time before suggesting them as an option and only offer up places that you know you can afford entirely. What we're not going to do is have you asking women to split the bill, or pick up the tip, or do anything at all that would require her to pay in any way, shape, or form. We're all very much aware what century it's and how capable women are of paying their way. That is precisely why it's your privilege to do it for her and show her just one of the many reasons why you would be an asset in her life.

I'm not going to argue about this. The man/masculine person pays for the date. Period. End of story. If you can't afford to pay, then you can't afford to date. Women/feminine people don't accept anything less. However, on the flip side, for women, don't take advantage of this, there will be more on that later.

Okay, so now that you're dressed, feeling good...actually, feeling GREAT, and you have arrived on time to the restaurant. When greeting in a dating scenario, a quick hug is ideal and removes the formality that comes with a handshake. A hug signals a more romantic tone while the brevity keeps things balanced and from feeling too intimate.

If there is a hostess at the restaurant, then they should walk first, followed by the woman and then the man. If there is no hostess, then the man leads the way to the table and, if he is extra gentlemanly, he even pulls the chair out for his date.

Just What the Doctor Ordered: How and What to Order on a Date

Okay ladies, I'm going to call some of you out: The purpose of you going on dates is not to get a free dinner. I'll repeat again: The purpose of dating is not to get a free dinner.

You know what? I'm going to say it one more time for all you folks in the back who are hard-hearted, hard-headed and hard of hearing: THE PURPOSE OF DATING IS NOT TO GET A FREE DINNER!

Just as if you were meeting for a business meal, it's a good idea to eat a little something before your date to avoid getting hangry. It's also a good way to not get hungry to the point that you're tempted to order up the whole menu, which is beyond rude, especially on a first date. Again, just like in a business meeting, the interaction is less about the meal and more about getting to know the person sitting across from you.

I've heard from men time and time again that women have taken advantage of the meal situation and it's downright disgusting. For example, I've heard about a woman who ordered so much food, including multiple entrees, that she could not finish it all and then still wanted to go to a second venue where she proceeded to order even more food!

Or the story one guy told me about a girl who ordered crème brûlée for dessert. She cracked the caramelized sugar topping, set the spoon down and continued talking. After some time had gone by and she still had not taken a bite, he asked her why she was not eating her dessert and she said, "Oh, I don't really like crème brûlée, I just like cracking the top."

I JUST LIKE CRACKING THE TOP????

Really ladies? Please don't be this woman. This woman is one of the ones who is making it harder for the rest of us. After having multiple experiences like this, I really can't blame men for feeling bitter and "some kind of way," because they are being taken advantage of and used in this manner.

Remember earlier when I talked about overall etiquette? This is part of what I meant. If you would not behave this way with a friend, family member or colleague, why would you do so on a date? Don't damage your dating karma by being a jerk.

It's a good rule of thumb to wait and see what your host orders so you can gauge what price point to either stay at or under. You can even ask the host, "What do you suggest?" or "What are you going to have?"

In short, two things need to happen to make this delicate balance of chivalry and fairness work: Men, pick a place that's appropriate for your budget; and women, don't be opportunistic jerks. Now, onto the meal, shall we?

Dine: Your Etiquette at the Table

Good table manners are a must in dating and in general. While you might not know all the intricate etiquette rules when it comes to formal dining, having at least the basics down should get you through most initial situations.

Don't chew with your mouth full. Say "please" and "thank you," and treat your wait staff with respect. Try not to order foods that are super messy or hard to eat. Not sure which utensil is used for which course? Start from the outside and work your way in. Use your napkin, elbows off the table, wait for everyone to be served before starting to eat, and ask for things to be passed to you instead of reaching across the table.

Everyone has varying degrees of dining training, and in the interest of helping your date feel comfortable, it's best to take the "When in Rome" route if you see that their dining skills leave a little to be desired. This doesn't mean if they are talking with their mouth full or committing some other egregious sin you should go down to their level.

However, if you notice they are eating boned chicken with their hands, then feel free to do so as well. This would not be the time to wield your knife and fork to deftly and perfectly devour your chicken using Continental Style. The three tenets of our etiquette philosophy are Respect, Honesty, and Consideration, and this would fall into the Consideration category. You would not want to make your date feel uncomfortable or embarrassed about their dining shortcomings, so it's okay to relax yours a bit to put them more at ease.

I know we're all super attached to our cell phones these days, but during a meal, they really should be kept out of sight. Ladies, leave it in your purses. Men, if it's too uncomfortable to leave it in your pants pocket, put it in your jacket pocket or leave it in your car. Only food and eating utensils should be on the table.

There are a few times when it's acceptable to use your phone during a date: if you're expecting a call, let your date know ahead of time that it might be coming in during your outing. When the call does come in, let your date know and excuse yourself while you take the call. Try to keep it to a maximum of five minutes and be sure to apologize and thank your date for their patience upon your return.

Another time where it's appropriate is if you're using the phone to look up something that comes up in the conversation. Say you're both going back and forth over what's the tallest building in the world. You say it's the Empire State Building in New York, and they insist it's the Shanghai Tower in China. It's perfectly okay to say,

"Hey, mind if we look it up?" One quick Google search later and you learn you were both wrong; it's the Burj Khalifa in Dubai.

Be sure to only look up that one thing though, as this is not an excuse to get distracted by any notifications or updates that may have come in on your phone. You use it to address whatever came up in the conversation and it then goes right back to its location.

Discuss: Let's Give 'Em Something to Talk About

It's usually advised to stay away from the topics of money, politics, religion or other potential fire-starters at dinner and other social gatherings. But for dating, I don't think any subjects should be off limits. After all, you're trying to get to know someone with the hopes of having a long-term relationship, so these things are good to know. I'll say it's important to know what to bring up when and where but honestly, it's never really and truly a bad time. I've heard it said that you can't say the wrong thing to the right person, and I tend to agree. Ultimately, if a person is into you and is someone you're supposed to be with, nothing you disclose will run them away. If it does, better sooner than later when you're halfway down the aisle and two steps away from saying "I do."

Generally, the first meeting, followed by the first actual date, tends to be more lighthearted where you're getting a feel for this person's vibe and assessing if there's romantic attraction and chemistry. The topics at this stage tend to be more surface level and autobiographical, where you're finding out about favorite foods and colors, number of siblings, hobbies, and work history.

By the third date things should be getting a bit deeper where you're asking pointed questions to assess areas that are important to you and your compatibility in a partner. If you're a person of faith and it's important that your significant other is as well, you should be asking about this by the third date. Same with their thoughts on marriage, children, Trump, etc.

In the event that something is disclosed that you disagree with, still keep your composure. If this is a deal breaker, take note, but no need to up and walk out of the date immediately. That is, unless they've said or done something to make you feel irreparably uncomfortable, offended, or unsafe. The key word here is irreparably. There will be many offensive moments, and I'm not suggesting you stay in a harmful or unsafe situation for the sake of being polite. That's what gets women harmed, to be honest. If you're ever feeling unsafe or uneasy, get yourself out of the situation. That said, when it's just that you've discovered something that makes you incompatible, go ahead and wrap up the date as you normally would, but know that you aren't going to pursue things further.

Here's a little tip regarding post-dinner bad breath. Carry a travel-size toothbrush and toothpaste with you or one of the little Colgate Wisps things–they're tiny one-use plastic toothbrushes that come with a glob of paste already inside.

I've found the best time to make a quick trip to the restroom for a breath refresh is right as dessert is winding down, but before the bill has arrived. If you're not getting dessert, then do it as the main course is coming to a close. You want to time it, so you don't have much left to eat, but not so late that your plates are clean and being bussed away.

Having fresh breath is imperative, especially if there's even the slightest chance of a kiss. Even when there isn't any kissing to be had, your breath will be minty fresh, and you can't go wrong with that!

When the bill comes, men, get it without any hesitation and take care of it without making any big show. Women, don't do the "fake reach" or offer to pay any of the bill. If he's truly a masculine gentleman, you making these overtures can actually be offensive to him. Men, after the meal is over, offer to walk the woman to her car or wait with her for her cab or Lyft, etc. to arrive.

So, the date is almost to the end but you're not home free quite yet. Now, it's time for the departure...but it doesn't have to be dreadful!

Your Behavior During the Date

During the Date DO's:

- Be on time.
- Say "please" and "thank you," and be respectful to the wait staff (another one of those overall etiquette tips).
- Follow basic table manners and make your date comfortable by following the "When in Rome" approach. If your date's manner of eating is on the more relaxed side of things, there's no need for you to break out your fancy etiquette skills by eating pizza with a fork and knife.

During the Date DON'Ts:

- If you're not the one paying, don't be rude and start ordering a bunch of things. Take note of what your host is ordering and keep your selections at or under that price point.
- Don't order messy or hard to eat foods like spaghetti, oversized burgers, crab or lobster.
- Leave the phones alone. Keep them off or on silent and give your date the respect of your undivided attention.

After the Date: Departure & Dismissals

Parting ways after a date can be among one of the most awkward moments in the whole outing. Do you kiss or not kiss? Hug or not hug? Want to see each other again or was this a one-and-done date? The approach is a little different depending on how things went and what you want moving forward.

When you'd like to see them again:

Sometimes there's sparks and you know this is someone whose company you enjoy, and you'd like to spend more time with them. Another quick hug is good here, perhaps with a little bit of lingering if you're feeling it. Ladies, I'm a fan of a quick peck on the cheek if it feels comfortable to you. Let the guy know you enjoyed the outing and would like to do it again.

Men, if you enjoyed yourself and want another date, it's great to let the lady know you'd like to see her again and check her availability to know when you can get together next.

When there's not going to be a second date:

Well, you win some, you lose some. Sometimes things simply don't click and that's perfectly okay! Be careful in these cases to not be disingenuous and make empty overtures of "we should do this again soon," etc. if you already know you have no intention of doing that.

Depending on the vibe, another quick hug might be had here. If your date asks to go out again and you're not feeling it, let them know right then and there that while you enjoyed meeting them, you don't feel like you're a good romantic match. As tempting as it is to do, resist suggesting that you "be friends" instead.

Ghosting is an absolute "no-no" for either party and the best way to avoid this bad behavior is by being upfront and honest instead of pretending to have some interest only to abruptly pull a Casper later.

After the Date DO's:

- Men, you can offer to walk your date to their car or wait with them for their ride to arrive.
- Men, do ask your date to let you know they made it home safely. Women, text when you arrive home (that's also a great opportunity to relay your appreciation for a lovely time).
- Be honest if you didn't feel a connection and let your date know in a kind way. A simple text at the end of the date works: "It was nice meeting you, though I don't think we're a good romantic match. Thanks again (for coming out/for a lovely time), all the best to you!"

After the Date DON'T's:

- Don't feel obligated or pressured into doing anything physical, whether it's a hug or kiss or even more at the end of a date if you don't want to. On the flip side, don't pressure your date to do anything they're not immediately comfortable doing.

- If you've already decided you're not interested in seeing this person again, don't make any empty "Call you later," or "We should do this again," promises.
- Women, as tempting as it is, don't contact the man first after a successful date. This is your opportunity to see if he's going to keep in touch because he really wants to and not just because he's responding to your call or text.

So, that brings us to the end of this chapter. I sincerely hope it's been helpful and has equipped you with a few more tips and tools on your dating journey. Online dating can be exhausting at times so don't be afraid to take frequent breaks from the apps whenever it gets overwhelming.

Also, be mindful of your expectations. Instead of obsessing over whether each new person you meet is "THE ONE!!" go easy and just think of each new person as just that: someone new you're meeting who could turn out to be a friend, business connection or perhaps something more. You never know and that is the beauty of this time. Hope and new opportunities are around every corner. Happy Dating!

The Termination of a Friendship

Elaine Swann

They were your partner in crime in high school, and you both vowed to be best friends forever in college. Now, it seems that such a promise was unwise since the two of you have grown apart and argue more often than you agree on things. A well-known quote, "Friends can come into your life for a 'reason' or a 'season'." You know that the time to part ways has come, but how do you break up with a friend?

Be gentle

It's not a bad idea to seek counsel from loved ones who don't know the friend you're planning to divorce. They can give you unbiased advice that can help you gently break the news to your former pal, always wishing him/her well in the future and honoring in remembrance your memories.

Let the end be the end

Politely tell your friend that your interests have grown apart, and the relationship needs to come to an end. Don't say that you need a "break" since you have no intention of reconciling in the future.

Stay away

Too many times people end a toxic relationship only to return to the person a few months later. Do yourself a favor and refrain from this behavior. You decided to bring the friendship to an end for a reason. Use the energy that you have reserved for reconciling to make new acquaintances. If you should run into one another at a social event, always be polite and cordial; but be careful about being pulled back into an ongoing relationship again.

Part Four

A Distinctive Approach To

Racial Issues

The Empathy for Other Cultures

Dr. Tumona Austin

Understand Mindset & Culture: How to move within a space that wasn't created for you

Is there a fixed-mindset, cultural tradition, or belief working against you? Are you aware of the various types of communication styles and different types of power roles? In order to go where no woman has gone before, you must do things that you have never done. You will encounter closed mindsets that are not open to you or accepting of your ideas along the way. In these instances, you want to take time to establish the WIFM (what's in it for me). By establishing WIFM, you create value and the opportunity to gain buy-in so your audience will be willing to hear your voice and be receptive to what you have to offer.

Infiltrating an Unknown World

When dealing with new cultures, it's important to exercise etiquette and to follow a modification of the golden rule called the platinum rule. While the traditional golden rule of "treat others as you would want to be treated" is a good starting point, it's an egocentric stance. It's presumptuous to assume that everyone wants to be treated the same way that you do. You're a unique individual with unique needs and unique desires. It's irrational to think that someone with an experience completely polar opposite of you and yours would want to be treated the same way that you would. In order to ensure that you were treating others with kindness and respect in a manner that they would like, it's important that you take time to learn about their culture, their individual needs, their customs, traditions, morals, and societal norms.

Culture

Culture influences the way we experience life and how we live, learn, and behave. It also plays an important role in shaping our personality. Customary beliefs, traditions, social norms/habits, language, religion, cuisine, music, and material traits of a group are all aspects of culture. Traditions and the unique variations across and within cultures are what make the world beautiful. Take time to appreciate different cultures (tolerance is not enough). Be aware of gestures and nonverbal cues and adjust accordingly. Be observant and ask questions respectfully. If you commit a faux pas, acknowledge and course correct. It's okay to inquire if you don't know the answer. Just make the inquisition respectful and ensure that you tie the question to a genuine desire to learn more. **Cultural appropriation** is the act of adopting elements of an outside, often minority culture (including knowledge, practices, and symbols) without understanding or respecting the original culture and context.

Mindset

Everyone sees the world through their own lens, and this lens shapes one's mindset. A mindset is a person's outlook on life and their framework for processing thoughts and information. Generally speaking, there are two types of mindsets: fixed and growth. A fixed mindset believes that qualities are fixed traits that can't change. A growth mindset is one of infinite possibility without limitations. Mindsets are powerful and have the potential to help or hinder. Take care to identify the mindset that you carry. It's important to understand the difference between the two types of mindsets so that you can take a step back and appreciate the lens that others view the world through.

As a powerful person, it's your job to uplift and empower others by respectfully challenging limited mindsets, within reason. A mindset of empowerment is uplifting, and it benefits all who encounter it. Empowered individuals look to make things better, to develop, to grow, to nurture, to think outside of the box, to develop novel solutions, and to identify problems that have yet to be detected. Engaging with people with limited mindsets can sometimes be frustrating. In those instances, take a step back and try to put yourself in their shoes. Engage with them from a place of appreciation, taking into consideration their circumstances and how that may have influenced their perspective and guided their interactions.

The Reality of Humanity

Elaine Swann

In March of 2020, we were all sent home from our businesses, schools, and organizations to hunker down during the COVID-19 pandemic. We were at the height of the stay-at-home orders and were all getting used to what we thought was going to be our temporary new normal.

As we started to get used to having to take our meetings via video conference and getting food delivered, in different ways, we were really getting settled in.

Then, eight minutes and 46 seconds happened.

For eight minutes and 46 seconds, all of us throughout the country were shaken by what we viewed across every media platform.

We watched a man by the name of George Floyd, lose his life right before our eyes. He was killed by a police officer who kneeled on his neck for that length of time. Against the pleas of a handful of bystanders, he remained in that position until Mr. Floyd eventually took his last breath. Usually, we don't see death in such a direct manner, except for in the movies where there's special effects and all sorts of Hollywood type efforts that go into it. But this time, it was real. A real, live man on the ground was pleading for his life and dying at the hands of someone who was supposed to serve and protect him. We watched as George Floyd called out to his mother and called out to the officer asking and begging for relief until eventually he could ask no more. He died, right before our eyes.

Then the protests started. The outrage that came with it whipped across not only our country, but all over the world. There was something that many individuals thought was dormant but became alive. It was the ugly fact that racism has always existed in our country.

Since this awful event, I often have conversations with individuals and have found that there are a few different categories of thought process about the existence of racism. Some thought that racism really had been dealt with and was something of the past. Since we had a Black president, this led many individuals to go through life thinking that racism was something that no longer existed and that it was gone from our country. The other category is those who thought that it only occurred in certain areas of our population and surely not necessarily their community, city, or state.

Once the conversations began to emerge, we learned quite clearly that racism unfortunately is still in existence here in our country. It is in our workplace, our communities, and unfortunately in our homes. The fact that we are having this conversation today tells me that we recognize that it does exist. Now so many of us are ready, willing, and able to do something to start to turn that curve and really deal with it head on.

We were all mortified by what we saw, but here is the thing that I think is quite unique: When we (the Black community) talk with our White brothers and sisters and have conversations about exactly what goes on in life, many of us share that this horrific tragedy is not an isolated incident. This sort of brutality is something that has taken place regularly for an exceptionally long time. The difference now is that it is being recorded and shared with the public in a very viral manner.

There was something that many individuals thought was dormant but became alive. It was the ugly fact that racism has always existed in our country.

The Exhausting Existence

Elaine Swann

I have dealt with racism my entire life. I am a Black woman, and it is part of just existing. Just as sure as I am breathing, I will surely be discriminated against for one prejudiced reason or another. As accomplished as I am, I too still must deal with the unfair bias that takes place in our world every day.

I am so thankful that I am very accomplished. I have gone from having my business as a sole entrepreneur, to building a company where we employ just under a dozen individuals. We have scaled the business with an incredible licensing program, and we now have over 20 independently owned and operated locations throughout the United States. I have had the blessing to be able to appear on shows like Dr. Oz, The TODAY Show, CNN, Access Hollywood, CNBC and countless others. I have presented to professional organizations and corporations such as Cisco, Merrill Lynch, and Bank of America. I have spoken at Wharton School of Business and Stanford University, and yet, I cannot escape racism in present day America.

One day, I decided to go out to lunch with a friend and we could not figure out what we wanted to have. While we were deciding by a fast-food restaurant, I said,

"You know what, let me go ahead and pop inside the 7-Eleven to grab a beverage to drink." Then my friend said,

"Well, I'm going to go through the drive-thru then," and since it was a nice day outside, I said,

"Hey, if it takes you a little longer after I make my purchase, I'll just stand outside and wait for you."

So, I did. I went inside, made my purchase, went outside and waited. It was a beautiful day, and the sun was out. I live in sunny California and it is not unusual to see a person standing outside. After a few moments, a police car pulls up directly in front of me. The officer gets out and starts walking towards me and says,

"Can I see your ID"?

I turned around and turned my head thinking, of course he couldn't be talking to me, I didn't do anything wrong. I was just standing there. Then his voice became a little bit louder and much sterner. He said the same thing again,

"Can I see your ID?" and I said,

"Yes, sir, absolutely."

I was a little taken aback. My first thought was to ask "Why?" but I was very timid and afraid to do so, because I knew.

I knew that, as a Black woman, any line of questioning from me could be misconstrued as aggressive behavior no matter how much I tempered my tone. I felt really anxious, but I mustered up the courage to ask,

"Officer, is there a reason why you're asking for my ID?"

I made sure to say this as I dug inside my bag because I knew if I were to dare ask straight up without being in motion, I would be accused of not being compliant and I could face severe repercussions. The officer answered by saying,

"Well, there's a rash of prostitution in the area and you fit the description of a known prostitute."

Now, in my mind, I'm thinking about everything I shared with you, and that I'm quite accomplished. I'm a pretty darn good citizen. I volunteer, I donate to nonprofits, I also sit on the board for nonprofit organizations. I own a business and am a job creator.

I wanted to say to him, "How dare you? Do I really look like a prostitute? This is broad daylight, and it's lunch time."

That's what I wanted to say, and that's what anyone in their right mind could have said, or at least questioned it in some form or fashion. But as a Black woman, I knew that had I opened my mouth to say a word to refute anything, I did not know whether or not I would make it home alive that day. That is the type of life that I live.

I was so humiliated. I stood there waiting while people went in and out of the store, looking at me wondering what I could have done wrong while the officer took his time. He took my ID, went back to his car and called it in and did whatever they did, to make sure I am who I say I am. I stood there, embarrassed, waiting with tears welling up in my eyes, but not wanting him to see me cry. When he finished with his checking, he handed me back my ID and said I was free to go.

Free to go.

As a Black woman in America. I am told I'm "Free to go."

Am I really free? Is this what freedom looks like?

That's the sort of reality that I live with every day.

Am I really free? Is this what freedom looks like?

The Exposure of Unconscious Bias

Elaine Swann

Two things were present in the story I shared about my exhausting existence:

Number one, is bias. It was clearly settled in the mind of that officer that my presence in front of the store was suspicious. He said so himself. It was insulting that he said I "fit the description of a known prostitute." What did that even mean? He obviously didn't see me as an individual, but only saw me based upon the color of my skin.

Number two, the lack of human respect and interaction. There was no conversation. No question of why I might be standing outside of the store. He got out of his car and immediately asked for my identification, which is something you do with a person who is being detained for suspicion of a crime or infraction. If the officer were to have taken a second look using his "trained eye," he would have surely confirmed that I was clearly not a prostitute.

I live in this skin every day of my life. I cannot take it off and put it back on. When you see me, you see that I am a Black woman. Unfortunately, there are times when people see the color of my skin and they treat me unfairly because of it.

This makes me think deeply about my dad, who immigrated here from Panama. He came to America in the sixties, looking for a better life. He was an educated young man and like every immigrant, he was seeking the "American dream." Years ago, we were talking about his early experiences, and he said to me,

"You know, I was treated so badly when I came here because of the color of my skin. Had I known that I was going to be treated so badly, I probably would not have come." So I said to him,

"Daddy, I'm so glad you did, and I thank you for what you endured because we really have had an incredible life."

You see, my dad served 26 years in the Navy, then retired and became an attorney, and retired again. I am very glad my dad came to this country because my siblings and I are all successful individuals and we live very fruitful and rewarding lives. I know it is because of the sacrifice, hard work, and determination of both my parents.

Too often, Black men have experiences like the one I shared earlier, yet we don't really talk about them to our non-Black friends and coworkers. We leave our jobs, have these horrible experiences, go home to tell our family, shake our heads and complain. Then we go back to work the next day and say absolutely nothing, because to us, it is a part of everyday life. I believe this is one of the reasons why many individuals thought,

"Racism doesn't exist here in the United States. It couldn't, it's gone."

Well, that is not true. What has happened is that technology has really helped shed light on what we are experiencing. Many of these encounters are now being filmed and shared on social media platforms so the information is being widely distributed. Now, we saw the extreme horrific circumstance happen with George Floyd, but there are many others that are very well-known within the Black community. It is important to recognize that there are some biases and stereotypes that take place that are not as graphic, yet are equally damaging. The Black community lives with them every day.

Unconscious biases are those social stereotypes that we may feel or show towards one group of individuals or another, for any given reason. The thought process towards others may not be incredibly harsh, but the effect of it is certainly unfair. Unconscious bias can be held against women or men, a particular race, or culture. It's an unconscious thing that we do that sets others apart from us in a discriminating manner.

The Solution for Change

Elaine Swann

One may ask, "What are the things that I can do to identify those biases"? Something to ask yourself, is there an unconscious bias that I have? If there is, what is it?

Use Your Emotional Intelligence

One of the things that we can do to put forth an effort to try to recognize this behavior is to tap into your Emotional Intelligence.

Ask yourself, why am I making this decision? Why am I going out to lunch with this individual? Am I spending more time with this particular coworker and less time with another coworker based upon the color of their skin or what I think about their ability or disposition?

We have to be conscious of what we are doing and how our choices impact others. We might have an individual that we're working with and we say, this person is not so good with numbers and I know this already because of the color of their skin.

Or you might say, this person is not so relatable maybe because of the neighborhood that they come from. Or perhaps, you'll introduce another individual to a program that you feel that they'll excel in because you believe they have an affinity towards this area.

Be conscious of what you're doing. Take a step back and really make an honest assessment on the choices you are making. For example, if you have to recommend someone for a particular job, position, or role; put together a list of candidates in a very practical way, and then evaluate that list asking yourself:

Are all the qualified candidates included? Is there anyone that I may have left off this list? Is there someone else that I should consider?

Utilize your Emotional Intelligence to recognize those biases and curtail the behavior when you realize it.

Blind Yourself

Another thing you can do is to Blind Yourself. Now, when I say blind yourself, I don't mean you should be color blind. I hear lots of individuals say,

"I'm color blind."

I will tell you one thing, that is not a good way to be. It is important that you see color. Color is vibrant. Color is wonderful. Color is what makes us different. We are all human beings, but our color makes us so unique, and you should see and appreciate each and every person for who they are and exactly what they possess. When I say blind yourself, I mean you should blind yourself in your decision-making. Blind yourself in the choices that you are making.

For example, if you're in the position to select a person from a list or an application, looking at the names of the individuals can be a telltale sign of the person's race or ethnicity. Blind yourself by covering up the names and focus more on their qualifications. You can do the same thing when you're making a choice whether or not to have someone join your organization. We must blind ourselves so that this way, we are really making an assessment based upon what

Dr. Martin Luther King Jr. said that one should be judged by the content of their character, as opposed to the color of their skin.

Increase Your Contact with Impacted Groups

Another way that you can help to bring an end to unconscious bias is to increase your contact with those groups that you have impartiality towards. If you find that you have bias towards Black people, then do what you can to spend some more time with them. Say hello to your neighbor, or you can take it a step further and stop to have a conversation with them.

Another thing you can do when you're in line at the grocery store or the bank, instead of just keeping to yourself, open your mouth to talk and say hello. Talk about anything, like the weather, how long the line is, or celebrity gossip. The more time you spend with the groups that you have a bias towards, the more you'll get to see that we are all human and all have many interests that may be similar to one another.

I am associated with a group called the North County African-American Women's Association (NCAAWA). The mission of this organization is set to assist Black women and Black girls by providing mentorship and educational scholarships. Although the group serves Black women, not all of the members are Black. We have members who do not look like us, and I tell you, we've had some wonderful, colorful conversations. We have been able to share and get to know one another. Our non-Black members have been able to ask questions and gain insight into the lives and experience of their fellow members. The fact that these ladies have increased their contact with women who do not look like them has helped them to eradicate any unconscious bias they may have possessed. As a group, we have learned to become sisters with the same focus and goals moving right along with one another, which is such a great thing.

Invest in the Future of Our Youth: 5 Steps

By investing in the future of the Black youth here in our country, we can deal with racism and unconscious bias in a meaningful way. It is important to recognize that much of the racism that is prevalent today is generational. Unfortunately, much of this country was built on the backs of slaves here in the United States of America. The slave owners treated Blacks like property and a commodity, not like human beings. The mentality of those labor owners was passed on to their children and their children's children. What we're left with is generations of individuals who had a terrible racist thought process and ideology about Black people. It was passed down from generation to generation, which is why we still see the remnants of it today.

As we get further and further and further away from that generation of racist slave owners, what we have is our youth of today and our future generations. I'm so hopeful for our young people and encouraged about the direction that they're going in. I believe they are the ones who will bring the dream that Dr. Martin Luther King Jr. and so many others had to fruition.

Today, as adults, we too can take part in the ideology of fairness among humankind. We have the power to help invest in the future of our youth. As adults and leaders in our homes and field, we have to make sure that we're putting forth an effort to develop into more of an anti-racist society.

Step One – Get Educated

Listen to real life stories, like the one I've shared with you. You'll learn that racism and unconscious bias is real.

Step Two – Set an Example of Tolerance for Others

Be intentional about taking opportunities to demonstrate that you can interact with folks that do not look like you.

Step Three – Be of Help in the Space That You Occupy, Whatever Space That You're In

If you are an authority figure, then utilize the authority that you have to demand fairness among everyone. Use the space that you occupy to set an absolute standard. You can intentionally say that you're going to treat everyone fairly, and then show it. When you see something unfair happening, step up and speak on the other person's behalf. When you witness bias or unfair treatment taking place, call it out. Don't do so in a harmful or disrespectful manner but be fair and firm.

Step Four – Create an Environment of Inclusion

If you are in a leadership position, stress the fact that your team needs to exemplify dignity and fairness towards everyone. Create an environment that is inclusive, that allows people to be included and be treated with absolute respect across the board.

Step Five – Lend Your Expertise to Those in Need

A very important thing you can do as an individual is to help the youth of our country for the future, and this makes me think about one of our Senators, Cory Booker. He has told this incredible story after Bloody Sunday (on March 7, 1965) took place where Civil Right marchers attempted to cross the Edmund Pettus Bridge. State and local lawmen attacked them with billy clubs and tear gas leaving many individuals injured and bloodied. A white lawyer who watched the march and the beatings on television was moved to act against racial injustice. He decided that he would dedicate one hour per week to donate his expertise as an attorney to assist those in need.

Mr. Booker's family was assisted by the Northern New Jersey Fair Housing Council to help them purchase their home in Harrington Park. They had a White family bid on their home on their behalf. The bid for the house was accepted and on the day of the closing, Cory Booker's father and the lawyer showed up instead of the white couple.

When Cory Booker's parents arrived with the volunteer lawyer to sign the documents, the realtor became very irate and did not want to finalize this home for the Black couple. The man even tried to punch Senator Booker's father and sic his dog on the lawyer.

In the end, the lawyer stood his ground on behalf of his clients, and they were able to purchase and live in that home. Cory Booker says that because he lived in that particular neighborhood, he was able to go to a wonderful school and be taught by incredible teachers who then helped him to get into college and now serves as a Senator for the United States of America.

That was a young man whose youth and the future of our country was impacted by the volunteerism of that attorney. So my advice to you is to lend your expertise in any way, form, or fashion so that we can help the youth moving forward.

You may not want to get out on the front lines and march with others, but anything you do in your community can help. For example, there might be a nonprofit organization that serves people of color and you learn that they're trying to raise money for a specific purpose, like trying to get computers or tablets for the organization. You happen to know someone in the tech industry that you can introduce them to. A simple introduction can create a world of difference for another organization. So whatever space you occupy, utilize the influence that you have to help others.

Making a Shift in the Workplace

Think about the places where you work and take an assessment of your workplace. If you don't have some sort of diversity policy in place, ask why not. If there is one in place, then do your part to get involved or help activate the agenda. You can check with the human resources management department at the organization that you work at to learn what's in place.

Don't just rely on HR but lean on yourselves as individuals to do what you can to make a difference. You can do a few things to be inclusive and make a difference in your workplace. You can include an employee of color in an important conversation. You can do this by directing an open-ended question to that individual or asking them for their opinion. When you are looking around to see who you can invite to meet a special client or key player, tap on the shoulder to someone of color, to invite them to come join in. These are just a few things that we can do to try to help close the racial gap.

The key for us to recognize is that we are all in this together. There's so much hope for our country and the fact that across our nation, we're having this conversation today tells me that we are on the right path. This is a journey that we are all on. It is most certainly not a sprint, but a marathon. We have to pace ourselves little by little and make tiny shifts and adjustments. We must do our part to stand up and speak out when we see unfairness taking place. Make sure that we stand in a gap for one another as human beings.

I was a flight attendant for many years and after the terrorist attacks on September 11, 2001, happened, we adopted a motto,

"If you see something, say something."

Well, that's what I'd like to express to you today. If you see something, say something. If you see someone being treated unfairly, whether it's in your home, neighborhood, or workplace, then say something. Let's all stand up and link together. As brothers and sisters in humanity here in this world, there's so much that we can do to help one another. And today is the day to start doing whatever you can to help close the racial gap here in America.

The Fairness from the Leaders

Deeran Anderson Hooper

Before we dive into etiquette equality, I would like to set a baseline and say there is a difference between someone who has prejudice and someone who doesn't value diversity. Although it's like splitting hairs, that small split is a HUGE difference. A person who is prejudiced looks down upon an individual or group and doesn't believe they are equal or worthy enough in that type of context. A person who doesn't value diversity, on the other hand, doesn't necessarily have to be prejudiced—it's more of a self-centered privilege of not seeing value in another way of thinking. Just to sum this up, remember that someone who doesn't value diversity will not be open-minded and will most times believe their way of thinking is better than the next person. However, they don't necessarily hate the other person or even think their way of thinking is wrong—just not as good.

It's hard to believe that we still need to discuss this issue and that there is still a need to march for equality, march against brutality, wonder if love will ever really be love, if women's rights ever be human rights, or if Black lives will ever matter not just in America but Corporate America to be more specific. When starting a new company or being in a growing one in today's time, hard conversations should be had. While it may be comfortable to discuss biases and prejudiced thoughts in an intimate setting among just your key players, a company-wide conversation may be necessary, which may call for certain etiquette.

In the small business and startup world, we all know that the work is limitless, but the manpower is limited, so everyone is working in close quarters and wearing multiple hats, which sometimes can be stressful. Now, imagine adding racial tension, sexism, ageism or any other type of prejudice to the mix. That dream you had of having the coolest workplace just went out of the window, and you're now seen as no different than the companies that were in the market before you. The reason why this is a bad place for you and your company to be is because the world is not a stagnant place. The world doesn't revolve around our growth and mindset, and since things are always constantly changing, it's up to you to embrace the changes and become one with the world. So many stagnant, failing small businesses are where they are so quickly, because they did not embrace the way the world moves forward at a rapid pace.

Some leaders are stubborn and don't go with the flow of society, business practices, or the community they serve. So, when you don't hang in our ever-fast-evolving social climate, you're actually digressing because the world will still move the way it wants to move with or without you. So, how do you as a small business owner or CEO of a start-up company evolve with the social climate and have these conversations with your team while also remaining true and authentic?

First, when someone brings an issue up to you, take ownership of the lack of awareness.

If you're not actively part of the solution, then you're actively part of the problem. Whether or not it's the pay gap between men and women, leadership equality for minorities compared to their white counterparts, or lack of diversity overall in the work atmosphere;

these are all different variations of systemic oppression that we all have or can participate in unconsciously. Therefore, your company and leadership must check in with your staff and clients often. When responding to injustice, take what your staff and clients articulated and acknowledge it without explanation or excuses. This approach allows for authentic ownership.

Second, don't make it about you, but make it about the cause or issue.

One of the main ways to take ownership of your part is that when someone brings up an issue about inequality, it's your job to respond to the injustice. Don't include messaging that emphasizes that your company has not known, or has not experienced something similar, or doesn't know what to say or do. The reason saying these things is a big misstep is because this leaves interpretation for dismissiveness to the issue at hand, which diminishes the whole purpose of your response. Remember the atmosphere of your company is not meant for you and people who look and think like you, but everyone involved in making your dream become a reality.

Third, have actionable steps in place for people to hold your company or brand accountable to the change you discuss.

After you have taken ownership of the situation, you now have to make swift corrective action—which means you can't just talk the talk, you need to walk the walk; especially if you want your team to continue to support your company's mission. Acknowledgment is excellent, but it's far from enough. Developing new systems, rules, and training to not only maintain quality but enhance inclusion internally is one step in the right direction. Another step in the right direction is donating money, lending your services, and sponsoring groups who are on the front lines of equality and that are near and dear to your team's heart. A final step is helping individuals affected by injustice reach a better quality of life through opportunities and mentorship programs with your company. Letting your staff and clients know these things are being put in place and revisiting them every six months to feel the tempo will allow you to see if you and your company are on the right track to becoming a brand worth standing by.

Fourth, value and diversity!

See how we circled back to this? The truth is that in order to be successful, one of the main things is to find and understand your weaknesses. This is where diversity comes into play big time. Once you know your weakness, you either address it and deal with it, or ignore it. If you ignore it, you know where that leads—just look at the companies now facing scrutiny—but to deal with it, you must make more decisions.

You will have one of two choices: build upon it, placing more minority groups in leadership positions in house, having more minority groups voices represented during the decision-making process, etc. Or you will build around the weakness which usually means "hire to it." This will involve getting someone else to build upon it, hiring a company diversity consultant, outsourcing certain tasks to minority run businesses, etc. Neither is better than the other, they simply require different approaches and executions.

This is why adding and valuing diversity can be one of the biggest and most important actionable steps you can do. It will help you do your best to mitigate becoming a brand or company that finds itself being insensitive to the times, staff, or company culture. As I stated before, you can do this by having a friendly, diverse group of people in leadership positions. Remember, adding diversity goes beyond managerial staff—it also includes executives, advisory board members, and outsourced positions such as consultants that you bring on board as well. Taking steps to make leadership diverse takes a conscious effort, because people naturally tend to gravitate towards people with similar traits and qualities to themselves. That gravitational pull may be acceptable behavior personally, but in the small business world, this can become very dangerous.

So, you don't get a pass for not having diversity because you say words such as, "I don't see color," or "I don't hire based on culture," as these can come off as dismissive in the first place. Seeing color and culture are not bad things, they are good things, because if you can't see anything, then how can you acknowledge it? The importance of knowing this is because those phrases lack acknowledgment of difference and result in invisibility, which means you're saying a person's color or culture is invisible to you and your company.

Fifth, revisit your mission and vision statement.

After you have acted, you also must do some reflection on the reason your company's culture took a turn or was not received the way you intended. Sometimes, that can come back to the intention at the company's inception. Take a look at your mission and vision statements, which are the words that embody the core of the company now and where it wants to go in the future. Like a ship out to sea, it's sometimes necessary to adjust while on course to your destination. The same goes for a person's brand or a company's mission and vision statements. As times change, societal and cultural norms adjust. So must your mission and vision if you still want to remain relevant when starting out. Ask yourself, do my mission and vision connect to or include verbiage that tackles the issues of society today? If not, consider re-working it so that it aligns with the evaluation of the community you serve. Let your customer and staff know the new update and why it has taken place.

Part Five

A Distinctive Approach To

Business

The Reliability of Professionalism

Benita Swann

Like a ship out to sea, it's sometimes necessary to adjust while on course to your destination.

Etiquette in the Office: Tips and Tools for the Workplace

My career has branched over several federal government agencies, through a series of traditional office settings and working with several supervisors over thirty-five years. Etiquette is the ability to adapt to various cultures, work environments, and working with people from around the world. Manners are not the sole reason for moving up the ladder. However, applying and knowing when to use etiquette can enhance your work style and move your career in the right direction.

Distractions are prevalent in the work environment; we can deal with some and ignore others. The way to handle many distractions is to maintain a positive disposition and learn to apply tips and tools of etiquette as you move up the career ladder. Etiquette improves communication with others, helps in handling personal distractions and manages emergencies that can enhance your career.

Personal Business on Personal Time

Personal Communication - (phone calls, texts, and conversations)

The work environment has changed a great deal from the workforce in the 1990s. Many employees today have a mobile device at their beck and call to check calls, texts, and post social media responses. Work areas have allowed employees access to mobile devices to take care of personal business at a minimum. Provided are some tips to be mindful of when working in the office around others:

- Be considerate when working around others while receiving incoming calls. If the call is unexpected, let the call roll to voicemail. Don't pick up the call in the middle of speaking with someone. It's always considerate to finish your discussion before taking a personal call.

- If you're expecting an important call that you must take, and your supervisor is near, excuse the interruption and let your supervisor know you must take the call.
- If a call can wait, that is great! Always check to see if the call is urgent. At the next break, take "a meeting in the ladies' room"
- Select a quiet ringtone or set your phone to a low vibration to prevent it from disturbing others.
- Put distance between you and your device. Tuck it away in the desk, so it's not visible to others.
- Wait to text or post on Facebook, Instagram, or Twitter. Since it's not a work task, it's best to text after work hours.
- Always return to the office from a call with a positive attitude.

Etiquette Tip: Watch your tone while working in the office. Personal calls sometimes make us relax and may lead to being loud. A good practice is to maintain your inside voice at a low tone to match your office's quietness. Set a good example by showing good office etiquette and getting off the call quickly.

Ensure that your tone is not distracting others in the office. Remember, this is not a personal space, and others may listen to share what they heard for the rumor mill. Maintain a soft tone and respect the etiquette of the office.

There is a responsibility that goes with the territory of handling private information, keeping it confidential and safe in the workspace. Don't leave public or private business documents when walking away from the desk. Tuck documents away inside your office desk and out of sight.

In an era of confidentiality and privacy, any discussion related to personal and private business information (PPBI) should not be discussed or shared in public areas with guests, visitors, or family. If you must take a critical business call during a non-business function, always excuse the interruption, and depart from the table. Avoid those listening by reserving a private booth ahead of time.

Lastly, avoid posting business information or property on Facebook, Instagram, or YouTube. Postings of this nature can lead to serious litigation for the company. All business entities have policies and practices when it comes to protecting private business information and property. Ensure to take an agency-related training course to enhance your company knowledge of confidentiality.

Handling Personal Emergencies

Life presents a multitude of unexpected situations, and we never know when such an emergency may arise. Some companies have family-friendly policies and work schedules for employees to support work-life. An emergency is an unexpected occurrence that can show up anytime. However, we can balance and manage emergencies that arise by developing a plan to deal with emergencies. For instance:

- Don't leave an emergency message with colleagues to share with the supervisor. This will help you avoid miscommunication and misunderstanding of information.
- In the event of an emergency, take a couple of minutes to communicate the situation with the supervisor to give them a heads up. Don't leave the office abruptly.
- If the supervisor is not available, leave a recorded voice message or email, advising them of the urgency, and update them later.
- If you're uncomfortable about sharing the details, just provide a courtesy call.
- Inhale, exhale, and clear all thoughts. Be present to deal with the situation at hand.
- Maintain a charged phone during emergencies.

- Personal distractions come in all magnitudes. Be calm, prioritize, and check to see if a response is needed. If the distraction can wait, wait for your next break.

Creating a list of emergency contacts is a helpful way to handle and focus on what is important in a stressful time.

Workplace Drama

The office setting is not the place for drama and sharing emotional baggage. Leave the drama at the door. Chaos, negativity, and verbiage should be left outside the work area. It brings confusion and uneasiness to the work environment.

- If someone reacts with offense, don't respond defensively. Make a TSW exit—thanks, smile, and walk away.
- Don't respond to an angry or annoying email. Close the email, take a break, and respond by calling the sender. Always avoid sending an angry email because it's harder to recall an email, than to make a simple call.
- If you need to acknowledge receipt of an angry email, respond in a short and brief sentence, "Thank you for your email. I'll get back with you soon." Research the matter.
- No, no, no, selfies at work! The workplace is not the place to post a response on Facebook, Instagram, or Twitter. A

selfie can capture an unexpected object or possibly other employees.

- Know when to hold and fold opinions. Keep arguments at ground zero while working in the office.
- Stay away from office gossipers—Make a TSW exit with a polite thanks, smile, and walk away gracefully.

Communication is a crucial component of the daily operation of any office. Knowing when to have a professional conversation can have a positive impact on career development and help you build relationships with colleagues. Communicating with respect and showing consideration for the sensitive subject matter is essential to fostering short or long-term relationships while networking along the way.

Handle Surprises at Work with Grace

Learn the Behaviors of Others

We meet many people in our life and during our career. Some are connections and others are disconnections. Occasionally, someone will surprise and catch us off guard. One can respond adversely or positively. One example and true story of surprising behavior, a senior executive walked into the office and made a comment, "Boy, you have big hair!”

It was like receiving an angry or annoying email. However, the same holds when professionals make unprofessional comments. Don't react quickly. Wait, like the process of receiving an angry email. Take a check in, inhale and exhale before you react. Most importantly, don't react in anger. Decide to respond gracefully and positively, excuse yourself, and check in with the person that made the comment privately.

Always take the opportunity to learn and understand how the leader is showing up. Always be considerate of others while working in the office. We can't stop unexpected comments and responses, but we can handle surprise comments with grace by showing leadership values of consideration, honesty, and respect for everyone.

Keep Facial Reactions to a Minimum

We all respond to surprises in different ways but knowing how to respond can be a gray area. Learn how to handle and respond with little expression and a lot of grace. An honest, forthright expression that is not dramatizing how you react is helpful as you learn to listen to others. It's good to check to see the temperature of the person engaged in conversation. Check in with your gestures to determine if the response matches the conversation of the person's actions. For example, if the supervisor is not smiling while sharing a personal outcome. It's probably not the best time to make smiley jokes. Be authentic and match the expression to what the other person is conveying. Usually, smiling is an affirmative action and receives a positive reaction. However, everyone may not smile. Check the mood with a "Good Morning," if the response is favorable proceed in a good way. If unfavorable, tread lightly, and attempt not to overreact with facial expressions. Again, learn from the behaviors of others.

Preparedness is Key

Be ready with a pen and pad, always ready to take notes for a meeting and showing up to be present. Showing up being prepared suggests a willingness to dig in and fill in where is needed. An executive office is continuously moving. Some offices have two individuals that assist the entire suite. In an executive environment, some leaders don't focus on the permanent staff. However, keep that pen and pad handy through all moments. You never know when that unexpected promotion is raised. Therefore, "Be ye also ready" (Matthew 24:44). Be patient, always be prepared with a pen and pad, and do your best, it all pays off.

Presentation Matters

Be on Time

Punctuality shows dedication, preparation, and respect for others while in a meeting setting. Showing up at a meeting allows employees to represent their office in a positive light. Punctuality is important because it shows dedication to the agency's mission, and preparation is needed to get the meeting organized for others. There are several reasons someone would be punctual, for example, to set up to ensure the food is delivered or ensuring that the technical equipment is working properly for the conference. Arrive early to network and exchange information before and after the meeting. No one can hide upon arriving late to a meeting, all eyes are on you. So, arrive on time, since it may be your time to shine.

Prioritize and Outline Your Daily Schedule

Review the calendar and check calls, outline and jot down all priorities for the day to stay on task. Schedule a 30-minute check in with your executive to advise of calls, meetings, and requests to determine if there are new tasks, or any scheduling entries need updating or amending. If unsure about a task, do take the time to ask questions to gain clear and concise directions. There is nothing wrong with repeating the question to make sure you understand the task at hand. Enhance your knowledge by taking training to refresh skill sets. Seek formal and informal mentors for career guidance and learn different experiences and perspectives.

Attire Matters

It's essential to consider dress attire while working in the office. Ensure the work attire is presentable to meet executives in the workplace. Evaluate yourself before leaving the residence. Listen to that sixth sense–if the attire is not right, and to prevent tugging at the outfit all day.

An Etiquette Tip: Leave a black jacket at your desk or in your office for unexpected meetings. Be aware of the office dress code policy on business and casual attire. Business attire is for business and night-life attire is for social outings. Be comfortable and confident in all business meetings. Respect the wear, and others will respect your attire. Respectfully.

Etiquette is adaptable in offices and cultures around the world. Communicate and handle all types of distractions and emergencies with grace by displaying leadership values of consideration, honesty, and respect toward everyone.

Knowing when to have a professional conversation can have a positive impact on career development and help you build relationships with colleagues

The Significance in Your Presence

Dr. Tumona Austin

Get their attention before you say a word. Walk into the room like you own it. You have the opportunity to command the room every time you have the floor. Come in the room, make eye contact, and acknowledge people as you encounter them. You change the energy when you enter a room, and you have a responsibility to manage and nurture that. Be aware of your use of language. Keep it positive, motivating, and uplifting. When people feel that they are recognized and valued by someone, they want to listen. Once you make an investment in people, they are more likely to appreciate that investment and want to engage with you.

To navigate a room, you need to walk around, interact with people, ask questions, and facilitate conversations. Make audible observations related to the context and material and acknowledge people's contributions and efforts. Literally move about. Moving throughout the room encourages your audience to not only follow the sound of your voice, but to track your movements; thus, allowing you to fluctuate the tone and projection of your voice. This allows you the opportunity to make gestures and conduct short role-play scenarios as well as other experiential learning activities to engage your audience. Additionally, you could stay still and instruct your audience to move. Navigating the room ensures that you achieve a good balance between being seen and being able to see the audience. Move around at a good pace and pay attention to your voice. Make use of careful pausing and, most importantly, rehearse. Your mindset and presence connect you to your audience. Make an entrance and channel your inner diva.

Dress to Impress

Adorn yourself from head to toe with confidence and arm yourself with a smile. Make a great and lasting first impression.

A few important tips for dressing for success:

1. Know the venue and the proper attire.
2. Dress for your body frame.
3. Take advantage of the psychology of color.
4. Establish a signature look for yourself.

Consider the following question: Is it better to be over or under dressed?

You can always take off your blazer/jacket to meet a situation, but unless you keep an emergency wardrobe in your car, it's difficult to add pieces to your outfit. Be the smartest dressed person in the room by managing your look with pieces that you can quickly dress up or down. What are some ways to quickly dress up or down in order to correct a dress code misunderstanding? Always overdress. If you're wearing a suit and realize the office is less formal than you expected, you can take off your jacket or some accessories to be more comfortable. However, if you start out in casual dress, there aren't too many options to quickly up-scale your look if you realize the engagement is more formal than you expected. Unfortunately, people do judge others based on appearance and clothing. If you're dressed formally, it shows effort and interest, even if you look out of place. Tip: keep a pair of heels or nice dress shoes and a jacket in the trunk.

Reflection: Ask yourself when you felt the most uncomfortable. Were you underdressed or overdressed?

Wardrobe Tips

It helps to have a functional wardrobe with timeless and multi-functional pieces. Below are eight suggested staple wardrobe items to empower you to look your best in any situation:

1. BLAZER
2. LITTLE BLACK DRESS
3. PUMPS/DRESS SHOES
4. BUTTON-UP SHIRT
5. KNEE-LENGTH SKIRT
6. WRAP DRESS
7. BLACK PANTS
8. PEARLS

Color

Color is powerful. Color can affect moods, behaviors, and stress levels. Research finds that certain colors yield similar universal impressions (for instance, the most statistically hated colors are typically yellow, orange and brown). Color provides a tool to allow you to be easily identified and further support your brand.

Additionally, types of colors (warm, cool, neutral) can evoke feelings. Warm colors give you a warm feeling and cool colors are cooling and soothing. Furthermore, it's important to be sensitive to the cultural significance of color. Some colors have various meanings across different cultures. You need to be aware of and sensitive to the cultural perceptions of color, particularly with respect to the audience you're working with. It's also important to stay current on color research because color significance, meaning and cultural variations can change over time. For example, green is associated with new beginnings, youth, health, prosperity, and eternal life in most East Asian cultures, whereas, in South American cultures, green symbolizes death. In Eastern and Western cultures purple is associated with royalty, wealth, power, and fame. However, in European nations, purple is associated with death and grieving. Gender differences surrounding color also exist. Blue is the most popular color for both men and women. The most unpopular color for men is brown. The most unpopular color for women is orange.

Apparel is a magical tool. You can change your colors to influence how others perceive you and the way that you feel. Questions to consider:

1. What colors are indicative of success and can give you the competitive edge?

2. What colors command attention?
3. Which colors are considered offensive and should be avoided?
4. What colors are you wearing when you feel powerful? Are there certain colors that make you feel less than bold?

In summary, color is powerful and may be used to do the following:

1. To change your mood.
2. To affect how others see you.
3. To influence and persuade.

The Sincerity in Evaluations

Nikesha Tannehill Tyson

Be sure that your goal is to be honest rather than brutal. Your motive should not be to hurt someone. Whether it's personal or professional, feedback can be difficult to both deliver and hear.

When giving Personal Feedback you want to do the following:

1. Ask yourself a few questions: Does the offender realize how they came across? Is the situation worth confronting? If not, take the high road and move forward. What is the expected

outcome after you address the person(s)? How serious is the matter, and will the relationship remain intact?

2. Speak privately, as you don't need an audience. Let's preserve the dignity of others as well as your own.
3. Ask questions for clarity before jumping to conclusions or making accusations.
4. Be kind and choose your words wisely. Refrain from attacking the individual with "you" statements.
5. Be specific and stick to the facts.

When giving Professional Feedback, you want to do the following:

1. Plan for a private location and time that works for both you and the other person.
2. Start with how the person contributes to the team or organization in a positive way.
3. Share your concerns.
4. Stick to the facts and be honest. Use the phrase, "My observation has been...," and use specific examples and times.
5. Refrain from using weak verbiage/phrases such as "I think," or "I feel."
6. Give action steps to help them move forward.

7. Refrain from being harsh. Your message is not likely to be heard.

8. End on a positive note.

9. Be sure to schedule a follow-up session. A person can walk away feeling empowered, even after discussing uncomfortable topics. The ultimate goal should be for the behavior to improve.

When you're receiving feedback, here are a few tips:

1. Be open and receptive

2. Listen.

3. Ask questions for clarity and for specific examples. 4.. Express appreciation (thank the person for bringing the matter to your attention).

4. Reflect on the feedback and commit to action steps to improve.

The Art of a Negotiation – There is much Power in Polite.

So, how do you get what you want or what you need in a situation? Be polite, charming, dazzle them with a smile, and then just ask. Be sure to call the person by name, (it gives a personal touch), and look them in the eyes. Think about what you want and the reasons why you want it. Be confident about what you're asking for in any situation(s) including your career, relationships, and business deals.

Whether it's personal or professional, feedback can be difficult to both deliver and hear.

The Confidence in Limitless Boundaries

Britney Lowery

"You're unique like everyone else."

This phrase is not only the opposite of a compliment, but it gives people the belief that they are not worthy or capable of global influence. Although the skill of decorum is vital, approaching etiquette as a language expands the relevance of it—far past cloth-covered dining tables, business networking events, and handwritten "Thank You" notes. Mastering this language, like any other culture-laced dialect, increases your realm of influence.

When you look at a globe, do you see just your street address? Your home state? The country you pledge your allegiance to? No, you see many, many destinations. Looking at a globe should do two things: humble and challenge you. Every person has the same potential to reach around the globe. As you learn your purpose and passion, know that there are people that count on your execution of it and those individuals live in multiple parts of the globe. Each culture has a reflecting one that crosses your home borders and surprisingly they are not much different than you. Build your brand by using the story of those places to inspire you and the framework of your purpose. Spend time getting to know their values, history, and pattern of influence they have around the world; all the while noting how you and your own story relates. Doing this directly connects to the foundations of etiquette, to your personal goals of influencing the cultures you grow attracted to. Setting the standard past domestic borders also challenges you to reach beyond your comfort level and propel you to accomplish more than you initially set out to.

"The sky's the limit," but if that was true, then how would we know of Saturn and Jupiter? The stars and galaxies? Even the Heavens? Just because our mortal bodies can't travel there, it doesn't mean we can't influence it. This is even more true for the future. It's comforting to think that we all will have 100+ years to live a slow-paced life pursuing absolutely everything we desire, at the rate that We're comfortable with, but that is not true. Wisdom and nature tell us to prioritize and be decisive. Once you pave your lane, refrain from setting boundaries on yourself. To better understand, consider this, in real estate, there are three realms of property rights:

1. Air Rights
2. Surface Rights
3. Subsurface Rights

Air Rights are connected to the air above the property. Surface Rights are those connected to land the property sits on. Subsurface Rights are those under the land where the property is. Take this and consider the concept of Purpose Rights. You're a Chef, and according to your Purpose Rights, you have the right to explore every culture of food, plant a few gardens, and maybe even discover new meal plans for astronauts. It basically means maximizing every depth and width of your lane.

When building a brand, there are two C-words that determine your brand strength: Collaboration and Competition. As we know, finding competitors is fairly easy, but pursuing collaborations can help you grow. Nature proves this every single day. Combining two fertile beings produces fertile fruit. Although, you can't always control the outcome, collaboration expands your influence far past what you could do as a solitary individual. Being open to partnerships and co-creation of things eliminates your lack of uniqueness, but it allows for you to celebrate what benefits the differences have to offer.

When you hold a globe in your hands, you have the physical ability to touch every border on that map—so how can that work for your influence? Housing the confidence and knowledge that the language of etiquette offers can help to fulfill and surpass your imagination, but it begins with dreaming, thinking, and learning of cultures outside of your own. Your simple respect of a place that doesn't yet know you is a sure key to unlocking your influence on that place.

Once you pave your lane,
refrain from setting boundaries
on yourself.